NATURE SPY GUIDE

SHELLEY ROTNER

Millbrook Press / Minneapolis

Anyone can be a nature **SPY.**

Here's how.

First you have to **GO OUTSIDE.**

Your eyes are good spies!
LOOK up.

What flies in the sky?

LOOK down.

TOUCH the ground.

OHHH . . .

LOOK all around!

BREATHE in . . .

SMELL the flowers blooming.

AHHH . . .

LOOK close. And closer.

And **LISTEN** too.

The sounds you **HEAR** can be a clue.

BUZZZ . . .

LOOK far. **LOOK** near.

Keep still. Animals might hear.

SHHH . . .

Take your time. **DON'T GIVE UP.**

Some animals like to hide.

RIBBIT . . .

And some blend in
or camouflage.

HOOT . . .

LOOK there! And there! I spy something red and round growing on a tree.

YUMMM . . .

Patterns, colors, and shapes

are everywhere.

Zoom in. Even more.

You might notice something

you didn't **SEE** before.

OOOH . . .

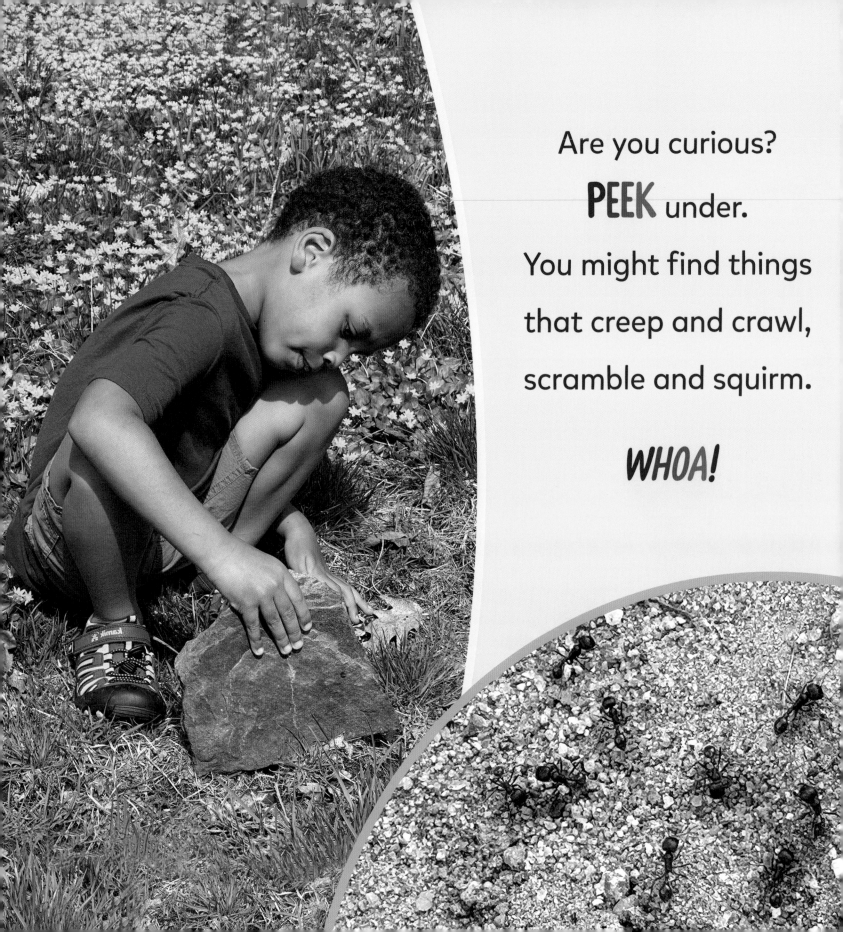

Are you curious?

PEEK under.

You might find things that creep and crawl, scramble and squirm.

WHOA!

Use your **IMAGINATION!**

Can you **FIND** letters or forest creatures

or cloud animals in the sky?

EXPLORE outside in any weather.

Anytime. Anywhere.

Now you are a nature spy!

PLANT AND ANIMAL IDENTIFICATION LIST

No spy guide is complete without a list of things you might find on your adventures! The plants and animals in this book are some common creatures you might find in the northeastern and midwestern United States. Some can be found across North America and in other parts of the world.

American bullfrog

ant

azalea

cottontail rabbit

earthworm

eastern garter snake

European honeybee

gray squirrel

great horned owl

mallard duck

maple leaf

monarch caterpillar

osprey

red eft

rose

IDEAS AND ACTIVITIES FOR NATURE SPIES

Spy tubes. Look through an empty toilet paper tube to focus on a small area. What can you see? Get close to a flower or moss on the ground, and practice using your spy tube. How does it change the way you see things?

Fingers full of sounds. Stand or sit quietly on the ground, and make a fist with one hand and hold it up in the air. Listen carefully, and put one of your fingers up for each different nature sound you hear. How many did you hear? Can you tell what made those sounds?

Sky frame. Cut a square out of the center of a piece of white card stock. Use blue crayons, markers, or paint (or all three!) to color shades of blue and gray in stripes on the sides of the frame. Then hold the frame in front of you and look toward the sky through your sky frame. But be careful not to look directly at the sun! Can you match the color of the sky to any of the color stripes on your frame? What else do you see? Any clouds? Birds? Flying insects?

Deer ears. Stand still outside. Do you hear birds singing, leaves rustling, or bees buzzing? Cup your hands behind your ears. Do you notice that everything sounds louder? Deer have large, cupped ears like this that capture sound. This is a good way for you to catch nature sounds too.

Color carton. Cut small circles out of colored paper, and glue them to the bottom of each circular section of an egg carton. Look for small objects in nature that match the colors in your carton, and place them inside. Try to find things that are loose and not growing.

Magnifying glass. It's fun to look up close. Your eyes are good spy tools. But if you have a magnifying glass, you will be able to zoom in close and make small things look BIG! When you use your magnifier, start by putting it close to the object you are looking at, and slowly move it up toward your eye until you can see the object clearly. What do you see?

Pattern keeper. So many beautiful patterns are in nature. It's fun to collect them to look at more

carefully. Take a ball of clay or homemade dough, and flatten it into a circle or square. This will be your pattern keeper. You can press a nonliving object such as a fallen leaf or feather into the clay and collect the pattern it makes when you remove it.

Do you see what I see? Look for an interesting shape, object, or scene outside that can look like something else— such as an animal or a letter of the alphabet.

Without saying what you are looking at, ask a friend if they see what you are imagining. For example, say "I see a white dog," when actually it is a cloud in the same shape as a dog!

Shape finder. Cut out a variety of shapes (such as triangles, hearts, squares, or circles) from thick paper or cardboard. Take a walk outside to see how many things in nature you can find that fit each shape.

Finding food. What kinds of food can you find in nature? You might visit a local orchard, a berry or pumpkin patch, or a community garden. Maybe

you can pick a healthy snack right from a bush, tree, or vine! Check with an adult to make sure you can eat what you find. Some foods such as blueberries have dangerous look-alikes.

Guess the nature item. With a friend or family member, collect some things from nature such as pine cones, bark, herbs, leaves, grass, flowers, rocks, or dirt. Then one person closes their eyes. Choose an item for them to smell, and see if they can guess the object!

Nature guest. How do you observe a living, moving creature safely? You can use a nature guest home! All you need is a clear container such as a plastic cup and a flat piece of thick paper or cardboard. Place the cardboard next to the creature, and let it crawl on top of it. Then gently place the cup over your "guest." You can observe it without spreading your germs, squishing any parts, or getting bitten! When you are done, gently place your guest back where you found it.

NOTES FOR CAREGIVERS AND EDUCATORS

Being outdoors in fresh air improves our physical, mental, and emotional well-being. Connecting with nature helps us to feel more grounded, to breathe more deeply, and to slow down, and see—to really see.

This book is meant to be an eye-opener—to highlight not only the beauty of nature but the discoveries and lessons "nature's classroom" has to offer.

Whether it's colorful flowers, animals on the move, or shapes and shadows, there's always something to see outside. The eye can be trained to look up, down, and all around—to look closer, again and again.

A connection to nature fosters a love and appreciation of the environment and all its living systems and creatures. It helps us understand the interconnectedness of our existence. Greater awareness of the natural world promotes future stewardship of the land.

Let curiosity, imagination, observation, and interaction guide your child's adventures to discover for themselves the wonders of nature. Anyone can be a nature spy! Take a look, and you will see.

FURTHER READING

Books

Bogan, Carmen. *Where's Rodney*. Illustrated by Floyd Cooper. San Francisco: Yosemite Conservancy, 2017.

Farrell, Alison. *The Hike*. San Francisco: Chronicle, 2019.

Goade, Michaela. *Berry Song*. New York: Little, Brown Books for Young Readers, 2022.

Lerwill, Ben. *Let's Go Outside*. London: Welbeck Editions, 2022.

Lloyd, Megan Wagner. *Finding Wild*. New York: Knopf Books for Young Readers, 2016.

Silverman, Buffy. *On a Gold-Blooming Day: Finding Fall Treasures*. Minneapolis: Millbrook Press, 2023.

Websites

Hitchcock Center for the Environment: Early Childhood Resources
https://www.hitchcockcenter.org/early-childhood-resources/

The Nature Conservancy: Partnering with Peek Kids
https://www.nature.org/en-us/about-us/who-we-are/how-we-work/working-with-companies/cause-marketing/peek-kids/

Nature Explore: Family Resources
https://natureexplore.org/family-resources/

Ranger Rick: Crafts and Activities
https://rangerrick.org/crafts-activities/

To everyone who loves and values the beauty of nature
to enjoy and preserve so we can have a healthy planet
for all living things. And to all the nature spies in this
book for taking the time to really look . . .

Acknowledgment: Much gratitude to Colleen Kelley for her contributions to the Ideas and Activities for Nature Spies. Colleen is the education director of the Hitchcock Center for the Environment in Amherst, Massachusetts. Hitchcock's mission is to create programs that educate people about the skills, aptitudes, and attitudes needed to care for our planet's ecological systems, build durable economies, and create sustainable communities. She has taught science in the outdoors to children for forty years and loves thinking and teaching about ways to integrate nature and education.

Millbrook Press™
An imprint of Lerner Publishing Group, Inc.
241 First Avenue North
Minneapolis, MN 55401 USA

For reading levels and more information, look up this title at www.lernerbooks.com.

Designed by Mary Ross.
Main body text set in Mikado.
Typeface provided by HVD Fonts.

Library of Congress Cataloging-in-Publication Data

Names: Rotner, Shelley, author.
Title: Nature spy guide / by Shelley Rotner.
Description: Minneapolis : Millbrook Press, [2024] | Includes bibliographical references. | Audience: Ages 4–9 | Audience: Grades K–1 | Summary: "What can you find in nature? Use all five senses to explore the outdoors. This guide is full of tips and activities to encourage close observation and foster connection with nature!" —Provided by publisher.
Identifiers: LCCN 2023021149 (print) | LCCN 2023021150 (ebook) | ISBN 9798765610152 (library binding) | ISBN 9798765610190 (paperback) | ISBN 9798765619261 (epub)
Subjects: LCSH: Nature—Juvenile literature. | BISAC: JUVENILE NONFICTION / Concepts / Senses & Sensation
Classification: LCC QH48 .R656 2024 (print) | LCC QH48 (ebook) | DDC 508—dc23/eng/20230630

LC record available at https://lccn.loc.gov/2023021149
LC ebook record available at https://lccn.loc.gov/2023021150

Manufactured in the United States of America
1-1009380-51689-9/13/2023